ISBN 978-1-334-27887-7
PIBN 10577988

This book is a reproduction of an important historical work. Forgotten Books uses state-of-the-art technology to digitally reconstruct the work, preserving the original format whilst repairing imperfections present in the aged copy. In rare cases, an imperfection in the original, such as a blemish or missing page, may be replicated in our edition. We do, however, repair the vast majority of imperfections successfully; any imperfections that remain are intentionally left to preserve the state of such historical works.

For support please visit www.forgottenbooks.com

English
Français
Deutsche
Italiano
Español
Português

www.forgottenbooks.com

Mythology Photography **Fiction**
Fishing Christianity **Art** Cooking
Essays Buddhism Freemasonry
Medicine **Biology** Music **Ancient
Egypt** Evolution Carpentry Physics
Dance Geology **Mathematics** Fitness
Shakespeare **Folklore** Yoga Marketing
Confidence Immortality Biographies
Poetry **Psychology** Witchcraft
Electronics Chemistry History **Law**
Accounting **Philosophy** Anthropology
Alchemy Drama Quantum Mechanics
Atheism Sexual Health **Ancient History**
Entrepreneurship Languages Sport
Paleontology Needlework Islam
Metaphysics Investment Archaeology
Parenting Statistics Criminology
Motivational

From the Board...

If You Feel Your Assessment Is Unfair
■ By Richard Emerson

Property taxes have become a major concern for all greenhouse owners. In the last issue there was extensive coverage of how property taxes may be set in your community. This issue will deal with the specific steps that must be taken if you should feel that the appraisal which has been set on your greenhouses is unreasonable. There are also set time limits which have to be adhered to.

Your first step is to make an appointment with the company who did the appraisal for the town. These hearings are set up in your town or city. This is your chance to get a look at your file to see how the figures were arrived at. If you do not agree or reach an understanding at this time, you pass on to the second step.

Your second step is to file for an abatement from the town. A form can be picked up from the Building Codes Officer in your town. Simply fill this out, return it within the specified period and the selectmen now become involved in the process.

At this point I should note that not only are you working within a specified time period but so are the selectmen. You should now contact the State Board of Tax and Land Appeals. They will

send you a form to file with the state and also a booklet explaining all the laws governing this process and the time frame everyone is supposed to work within. There is a fee involved in this part of the process.

If you still are unhappy with your assessment and you have filed your form with the state, you now sit back and wait for an assessor from the state to visit you. This is a long process (about 9-12 months). During this time you must pay your property taxes.

Once the state assessor visits you he will make a recommendation with the State Land and Tax Appeals Board for a hearing. When a date is set for this, you will have a hearing with not only the State Board but also a member of the company that did the appraisal as well as an officer from your town will be present. Hopefully a settlement fair to all involved will be reached at this time.

Your final chance of satisfaction is with the courts. Hopefully you will never reach this point. The sooner in the process that a reasonable assessment can be agreed upon the better. The process can be stopped by you at any time. Though you may find it difficult, try not to do battle with the people in your town on a personal level.

One more point should be made.

Even though it will cost you money, you should hire a lawyer knowledgeable in this process. He will make sure you understand what, when and why you must do everything that you will have to do in order to reach a successful conclusion to the property tax issue. You must make sure that you follow his advice. You can be sure that the other parties involved will have legal counsel. For these reasons, the money to hire the lawyer should be money well spent. I know the process seems very involved. However, there is one big factor in your favor: going into it, you should know more about greenhouse construction and how much you have put into it than anyone else involved in the process. If you follow the right procedure and try to be reasonable, things should work out in your favor. It's only right!

Also, the dates of the 1990 New England Greenhouse Conference are October 22 through October 24. Extensive planning has gone into this conference in order to make it interesting and educational for anyone connected to the greenhouse industry. I am sure that you will find it not only informative but also entertaining. See you there!

Richard Emerson owns Emerson Avenue Greenhouse in Hampstead, NH.

Board Meeting Minutes
September 5, 1990

The meeting, held in Barton Hall at UNH, Durham, came to order at 7:10. Alan, Chris, Jennifer, Kirk, and Richard were there.

July's minutes and the current financial report were read and accepted. Correspondence was read and discussed. A suggestion by B&E Supply that the association purchase a photo album in which to keep pictures of its various displays and functions for future reference was seen as a good idea.

The summer meeting—and ways to improve it in the future—was discussed and plans for the winter meeting were formalized.

The winter meeting will be held on January 17 at the Margate in Laconia. The program will begin around nine with a brief business meeting. Speakers will include Richard Zoerb from Gloeckners' giving an update on new items being sold in the New England area and Tom March discussing small engine maintenance. The featured speaker will be Donna Singer, an organizational consultant specializing in employee/management training and human relations in general. Her topic will be geared specifically toward employee/employer and family situations within the industry.

There was a general discussion about the Plantgrowers' Association displays—at the New England Greenhouse Conference, the New Hampshire Farm & Forest Show, the Granite State Garden and Flower Show: their usefulness; how to improve them; how

to get better publicity from them. Alan Eves is going to look into buying new panels for the current display.

There was also a discussion about membership recruitment and it was decided to come up with specific ideas for next month's board meeting—which will be held on October 3 at 7:00 in Barton Hall.

The meeting adjourned at ten.

Welcome New Members...

Wales Nurseries, Inc.
P.O. Box 158 Peck Road
Wales, MA 01081

Dr. Stanley R. Swier
Nesmith Hall
University of New Hampshire
Durham, NH 03824

3

In the News

New Hampshire News

New Glass House in Loudon

D.S. Cole Growers on North Village Road in Loudon, is putting up a large and—for this area—unusual house. The house is glass. The four-bay, 17,000 square foot house with venlo-style roof is manufactured by Verbakel-Bomkas, a Dutch company with American representatives in Atlanta. Because the gray weather in Holland demands houses that give the plant as much light as possible, many new houses there are glass. In New Hampshire, that's not a requirement.

"But glass seems a better total environment," Doug Cole, owner, says. "Lack of drip, better light, long-term low maintenance—these things are important." We looked out at the line of nine quonset houses going back from the farmhouse. "For immediate financial return, quonsets are a smart way to go. But with the new house, I feel I'm building for the future."

The new house—state-of-the-art in many respects—is surprisingly simple. The sides are a double layer of glass, the roof, single. There are no fans. Air circulation is supplied by vents alone—small ridge vents and huge end vents that open up and allow benches of plants to be moved outside on warm spring days to give sunlight to other plants being grown on the ground below them. The boiler uses a duel oil/natural gas system; there is overhead heating and bottom heat for the benches.

It's a year-round house—an overhead shading system used for protection from the summer sun is also used as a thermal screen on winter nights. The house can be partitioned into specific heating zones, or when the range of temperature required is not too great, kept as one unit in which the temperature in one area is modified slightly.

Many aspects of the house's operation are computerized. Both the computer and heating capacities are purposely oversized—ready to accomodate future expansion.

"I'm not quite sure how it will work," Cole says. "I guess we'll find out." Poinsettias are growing there this fall.

A New President...

At the August 15 Board Meeting of Granite State Garden and Flower Shows, Inc., John Jacobs was nominated and elected President for the coming year. John owns Mr. Bee's in Hooksett.

Also at the meeting, Don Gagne volunteered to handle the judges for the 1991 Manchester show. Possible exhibits include a garden designed for the handicapped, a tropical garden, and a display of Acacia trees. Many ideas for an overall theme were discussed, but none was chosen.

Anyone interested in renting space for a booth should contact John at Mr. Bee's—(603) 627-7667; anyone interested in space for a garden exhibit should contact Booth Hemingway in Kittery Point, Maine. His number is (207) 439-2241.

A New Show...

The New Hampshire Landscape Association has announced the first annual New England Landscape Exposition to be held March 14 and 15, 1990, at the Center of New Hampshire Holiday Inn and Convention Center in Manchester. This is an industry-oriented show for New Hampshire landscapers.

Aspects of the show include a trade fair, raffles, educational lectures, and pesticide recertification credits. For more information, contact Guy Hodgdon, 18 Debbie Lane, Eliot, Maine, 03903. The telephone number is (207) 439-5189.

And a New Chair of Plant Biology at UNH

On October first, Dr. Curtis V. Givan became the new Chair of Plant Biology at the University of New Hampshire. He also has the rank of Professor with tenure.

Dr. Givan was born in Sacramento, California, in 1939, studied at Stanford, and received his doctorate from Harvard in 1968. The title of his thesis was

"Regulation of Respiration and Glycolysis in Cultured Cells of *Acer Pseudoplananous L.*"

He was most recently Program Director of the Cellular Biochemistry Program of the Division of Cellular Biosciences of the National Science Foundation, Washington, DC, and—concurrently—senior lecturer at the Department of Biology at the University, Newcastle upon Tyne, United Kingdom.

Although his appointment may have no immediate effect upon the plant growers of this state, his actions as Chair of the Plant Biology Department could be of long-term importance to the industry. We wish him success in his new position.

Workshop Offered

A one-day workshop entitled "Workplace Safety/Health: Planning, Protection, and Compliance," sponsored by the UNH Cooperative Extension, the New Hampshire Safety Council, the Farm Family Insurance Companies, and the NH Department of Labor, will be held in three locations in the state this fall.

It will be held on Thursday, Ocober 25, at the Lancaster Town Hall on Route 3 in Lancaster; on Tuesday, October 30, it will be held at the NH Technical College on Route 120N in Claremont, and on Thursday, November first, it willl be held at the Belknap Mill—next to City Hall–in Laconia.

Topics include OSHA Compliance, Personal Safety Equipment and Practices, Legal Liability, and Employee Training Techniques. Three credits will be granted to people attending for the core category for 'Commercial Pesticide Applicator for Hire' and 'Commercial Pesticide Applicator Not-for-Hire.'

The cost is $25.00, which includes lunch and breaks. Registration should be sent to: NH Safety Council, 105 Loudon Road, Concord, NH 03301, by October 10. For further information, call (603) 228-1401.

4

Elsewhere In The News

EPA Pesticide Line

The Environmental Protection Agency (EPA) has established a toll-free number for pesticide information. The number is 1-800-858-PEST. The service, operating from the Texas Tech University (Lubbock) School of Medicine, operates 24 hours a day, seven days a week.

There were no computerized messages. Friendly, down-to-earth people told me that information given was "a little bit of everything"-safety, toxicity, regulations. They do not tell you what works on what—they don't give information on pest control.

But they are busy—they've had over 36,000 calls this year ("it slows down around Christmas"). The calls come from all over the United States, with the largest numbers coming from New York, California, Massachusetts, and Texas.

Oils Face Uncertain Future

Horticultural oils could face an uncertain future in EPA reregistration process, AAN learned recently. Concern over potential data requirements for these highly refined oil products, which are critical cornerstones of nursery integrated pest management programs, has prompted major horticultural oil producers to form an "oils task force" to cooperatively develop data necessary for reregistration. AAN will continue to monitor the situation.

Does Rockwool-amended Media Improve Growth?

North Carolina State University scientists tested plant response and nutrient uptake of seven plant species in media with and without rockwool. A mix of 20 percent rockwool; 10 percent peatmoss; 20 percent vermiculite; 45 percent pine bark; 5 percent perlite resulted in significantly better growth on impatiens, marigold and petunia than plants grown in either of two commercial media. Chrysanthemum, geranium and poinsettia growth was better in the commercial media in one half of the trials. Differences in growth weren't related to plant nutrient composition.

Blue roses-why not?

Calgene Pacific, a California biotech company, is currently working on inserting the blueness gene from petunias into a red rose. Apparently, cut flowers with unusual colors are very successful in Japan. A Japanese food and beverage company, Suntory Ltd., is funding the project to make the insertion of a variety of genes routine.

Argus Develops Computerized System

After 12 years of research and field experience, Argus Control Systems Ltd., White Rock, British Columbia, has developed a high performance computerized greenhouse control, alarm and data logging system specifically for North American growers, greenhouses and climatic conditions. Standard features in the climate, irrigation and nutrient programs provide substantial improvements in crop quality and yield, while simultaneously achieving savings in energy, water and fertilizer use, says Alec Mackenzie, manager.

The Argus Computer Control System is a distributed control system providing high reliability and easy installation and maintenance. It consists of one or more central computers situated in the greenhouse or in the home and individual controllers in the greenhouse. When not being used to view greenhouse operations, the IBM-compatible computers can be used to operate other software programs. Its modular design minimizes installation costs and allows easy expansion, while offering resistance to major failures, as each system operates individually. Many service problems can be carried out by the greenhouse staff by a simple board replacement.

Government research stations, educational institutes, commercial floricultural, vegetable, nursery and tree seedling producers in the United States and Canada are using the Argus Computer Control System. Argus can provide complete turnkey installations, or assist growers in installing the system in new or existing facilities. For more information call (604) 538-3531.

New Insectary to Open

In a matter of months, depending on the success of trials and the production of a new parasite for sweetpotato whitefly, floral growers may have a new weapon for one of the industry's most common and difficult-to-control pests. American Insectaries, Escandido, California, is preparing to produce sweetpotato whitefly parasites of Eretmocerus genus, although three parasites are presently under study.

The eretmocerus parasite was imported from the Middle East and released into the wilds of California 6 years ago. Since then, Jim Davis, American Insectaries president, along with several entomologists, have been monitoring the success of the release. Earlier this summer, they returned to the monitoring area and collected specimens from the original release site and are presently field trialing the parasite in commercial floriculture-producing greenhouses, as well as in other agricultural areas.

"Eretmocerus parasites have great potential for all of agriculture," Jim says. "Sweetpotato whitefly is a widespread pest that's difficult to control. Encarsia formosa will parasitize the nympha 2 stage of sweetpotato whitefly, but sweetpotato whitefly is not the parasite's primary host, making control difficult. I feel eretmocerus will be a better control agent, and our initial studies look very promising."

-Grower Talks Magazine

5

6

A Review of IPM Tactics

■ by Dr. Stanley R. Swier

IPM is a new buzzword heard more and more throughout the horticultural industry. Integrated Pest Management is simply the use of a variety of techniques to reduce pests without the sole reliance on any one (i.e. pesticides). The exclusive use of pesticides to control pests is no longer an acceptable option for political, sociological, and biological reasons. There is a tremendous fear of pesticides by the public. Although this fear is exaggerated, the perception is that all pesticides are extremely dangerous. In this case, perception becomes reality and it is difficult for the industry to fight it. In addition, the concern for protecting groundwater, endangered species, the environment, and human health all translates into tougher state and federal regulations of pesticides. The cost of developing and registering a new pesticide is now around 40 million dollars. Due to the small market of the nursery and greenhouse industry, few new pesticides will be available to replace those we are losing. Those pesticides which remain in our inventory, are becoming useless due to insect resistance. Therefore the wise manager will not rely solely on hard pesticides and will look to other methods to prevent pest buildup. Admittedly, IPM in New England ornamentals may be more difficult because our industry is composed of many small family operations. For economical reasons, these operations are overcrowded, contasin a wide variety of plant material, and have an uneven turnover of plants. However, we must try to do better to implement IPM. Many of the following suggestions are nothing new, but too many growers are forgetting the basics. I will also point out the problems you will face in trying some new IPM tactics.

Exclusion and Sanitation:

It is easier to prevent pest problems by not allowing them into your greenhouse or nursery than to try to control them after the population explodes. Not enough time is spent on inspecting plants before you accept shipment. After the plants have been in your possession for awhile it is difficult to prove they came infested with pests. Greenhouse vents should be screened. The new spun bonded materials will keep out the smallest insects but they do reduce air circulation. Weeds in and out of the greenhouse become an excellent reservoir for reinfestation of insects and mites. Eliminate weeds immediately outside of greenhouse walls, doorways, or side vents. Don't forget to destroy old plant material and fumigate between crops to destroy any leftover insects.

Biological Control:

Biological controls vary from those that are simple to use to the very complex. The simplest are those that are used like pesticides. They are stored until needed, mixed up, and then applied. Bacillus thuringiensis (Dipel, Thuricide) is very effective against many caterpillars but is very short-lived and frequent applications are necessary during a prolonged outbreak. For some species, only the young caterpillars are controlled by Bt, so proper timing is very critical. Bacillus thuringiensis israeliensis (Vectobac) has been shown to be effective against fly larvae such as fungus gnats and shore flies. BTi can be easily applied through the irrigation system.

There are several species of nematodes which are available commercially that can be used against soft-bodied insects such as grubs and caterpillars. These species of nematodes only feed on insects and do not harm the plant. Presently, nematodes work best in containerized plants against soil pests such as the black vine weevil. The routine use of nematodes has been hindered by high cost, poor storage ability of the formulations, high soil moisture requirement, U-V light sensitivity of the nematodes, and erratic performance. Further research will solve many of these problems and nematodes will gain wider acceptance. The use of nematodes will require that the grower refrain from using other pesticides which may be harmful to them.

Some species of fungi are specific to insects and are already commerically available (Vertalec, Mycotel.) Fungi can be very effective against aphids and whiteflies but have two disadvantages. They require high humidity which encourages plant pathogenic fungi and fungicides used to control plant diseases will adversely effect the insect pathogenic fungi. In order to use these pathogenic fungi properly, high humidity and altered fungicide schedules are necessary.

Interest in predators and parasites is increasing. The use of these organisms is very complex because they have specific environmental and host requirements. Predators and parasites tend to work best under the following conditions; 1) only one or two crops are being grown to simplify logistics; 2) crops are longer term in order to give the biological control agents time to work, 3) there are few other insects on the crop because spraying for other insects kills the biological control agent; 4) to appease consumers, the biological control agent is not present (its purposely killed with insecticides before the plant is sold, or does not usually appear on the plant product sold (i.e. greenhouse tomatoes); 5) the grower is willing to thoroughly understand the complex relationship between the plant pest and control agent and 6) willing to devote the time to alter the environmental conditions, chemical control program, and crop production practices to make biological control work. Not all pests can be controlled by biological agents. Some, like cyclamen mite, require preventative chemical control.

Soft Pesticides:

As traditional insecticides become less effective and more expensive, there is more commercial interest in developing alternatives. Safer's soap can be used against a wide variety of insects. However, to be effective, thorough coverage and frequent application is necessary. A horticultural oil is now available for greenhouse use. Sunspray Ultra Fine Spray Oil was recently registered in New Hampshire. We need to increase our use of horticultural oils in both the dormant and growing season. Unfortunately, much prejudice exists against oils because the old style oils

(continued from previous page)

were heavy and contained impurities which caused plant injury. Modern oils are lighter, purer, can be used all year long and are much less likely to injure plants. Still, horticultural oils like any pesticide should be tested on a few plants first, especially in hot weather. Oils tend to kill insects predominately by suffocation and are most effective against eggs and juveniles of mites, aphids, scales, and mealybugs. Neem (Margsan) is a seed extract which is new to the marketplace and not yet registered in New Hampshire. It has been effective against greenhouse leafminers and further uses are being developed. Abamectin (Avid) is a macrocyclic lactone that is labelled for mite control but also effective on many other insects.

Resistant Plants:

Many varieties of plants are naturally resistant to certain insects. Grow-

ers and landscapers should encourage the consumer to buy resistant varieties. Unfortunately this is easier said than done as consumer preferences are often dictated by physiological traits and cosmetic appearances. As long as pesticides are still relatively cheap and easy to apply, there is little incentive to change. However, as environmental concern increases, consumers will demand low maintenance plants.

Monitoring and Mechanical Control:

Not enough use of yellow sticky boards occurs in New Hampshire. The insect is attracted to the yellow board and is trapped by a sticky substance. You must determine if its worth making the boards yourself or buying them. The boards will attract aphids, whiteflies, thrips, and fungus gnats. The boards don't have to be large, but should be 2-4 inches above the plant height. One trap placed every 30 square feet

will reduce insect populations considerably. If traps are used just to monitor insect populations, fewer are needed. Traps should be checked at least once a week. Chemical controls should be applied when damaging insects first appear as it is far easier to control insects when populations are low. The most common error growers make is to wait too long to initiate control. Once an insect population has erupted, control is difficult even with chemical pesticides.

Dr. Swier is an Extension Specialist in Entomology. for further information on IPM, you can write Dr. Stanley Swier, Nesmith Hall, UNH, Durham, NH 03824, or call him at (603-862-1159).

9

Pricing For Profit

■ By Tina F. Sawtelle

Has this ever happened to you? Customer: "Oh, how darling!" picking up item to note the price. No price is apparent. She quickly sets the item back down and moves on.

Problem: Merchandise not priced clearly and customer is not motivated enough to ask.

Result: Failed impulse purchase. Decreased profits for the day. Chances are it may happen more than you realize. And it's not always with small priced items! Review your pricing techniques using the following tips:

Straightforward Pricing

Make it easy for the customer to buy! Price items leaving no question in the customer's mind. For example, for a 25% off sale, is it clear if the price already reflects the 25% off or is it 25% off the marked price? Be objective and look at pricing from the customer's standpoint.

Make Sure Everything is Priced

As a routine management procedure you should have your employees checking that all items are priced accurately at all times. Pricing can be done individually or as a group on items such as plants. Check for signage that has been moved or removed, tags that have fallen or are hidden. Customers will pass by an item they are unsure of pricing on rather than ask.

Clear Pricing

Are the tags legible? Are they faded or washed away? Are the tags reachable (on hangers for example). Are the prices in an area that can be easily seen? A tag under foil or buried inside a plant is not accessible.

Price Does Not Detract From The Product

Pricing can be clear without detracting attention from the product itself. A beautiful white Poinsettia can lose appeal with a bright orange tag hanging off the flower of the plant. A much more subtle but clear and straightforward approach will be effective.

Use Odd Ending Pricing

$9.95 or $9.99 always sounds less expensive than $10.00 The increased sales from this method of pricing will pay for the inconvenience of making change in the long run.

Be Complete

If you are displaying two items together in a suggestive manner, be sure to be complete in your pricing. Price as a package or clearly price each item separately, to avoid frustrating the customer.

Offer Multiple Pricing

Offer your customers volume discounts to encourage larger sales. It works! $4.99 each or 4 for $18.99. The discount need not be excessive, but the suggestion of multiple purchases works with customers. If you have shown uses for that multiple amount it works exceptionally well.

Discount Policies Clearly Stated

Will you offer Senior Citizen discounts to build this growing portion of the market? Is you policy clearly posted and do your employees understand the policy? Are there any other special interest groups you will extend discounts to?

Employees Know Prices

Your employees should be aware of all prices so if a question arises they can handle it. You can't expect to sell your merchandise if you can't tell the customer what you want in exchange for it. Have some policies stated so that your employees can make sound decisions when faced with questions.

Remember in business, "Nothing happens until somebody buys something." Make it easy for your customers to buy! Good luck!

Tina Sawtelle, principal of Sawtelle Marketing Associates, consults with Agricultural Direct Retail Businesses on marketing and merchandising. In addition, she teaches Agricultural Business Management techniques to students at the Thompson School at UNH. For more information call (603)659-8106.

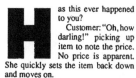

12

Opportunity Is Knocking

■ By Cal Schroeder

Have you ever wondered what kids think about your profession? Maybe what they think about agriculture in general? With instant and processed food, plastic trees and flowers, imitation this and that, kids often form unrealistic impressions. The Agriculture In The Classroom (AITC) program is trying to change mistaken impressions into true concepts.

AITC is a national effort originating from the United States Department of Agriculture but conducted by each state individually. The purpose of the New Hampshire AITC program "is to enhance the understanding of agriculture among K-12th grade school students throughout the state, leading to a new generation of knowledgeable citizens who can make judicious decisions about agriculture."

How can our legislators, community leaders, or the general public itself vote for continued use of pesticides, protection of agricultural land, or advocate for the use of public water for irrigation if they never learned the importance of a local agriculture?

The N.H. Agriculture in the Classroom Council was formed for just that purpose. The goals of this organization are:

1. To promote an understanding of the political and economic relationship between agriculture and society.

2. To develop an understanding of nutrition and other health issues.

3. To increase knowledge of food and fiber production.

4. To enhance the image of modern agriculture.

5. To develop an appreciation of our historical heritage.

The Council has hired a part-time coordinator. Her name is Laurie Bryan and she has an office at the N.H. Farm Bureau on Loudon Road in Concord. She needs your educational and financial support.

Have you ever thought about the good you could do for your profession by speaking to a class of students? Sharing with them some of your knowledge of how plants grow? What it takes to keep plants healthy? Maybe a tour around the school identifying trees and shrubs will provide kids with an appreciation that plants are living things needing their care. For older students, a visit to a job you're working on might create an interest in them that may lead to potential employees in the future.

As an organization, the N.H. Plant Growers has mainly supported activities pertaining to high school and college-aged students. Maybe the opportunty is now available to influence many more students–elementary youth. When kids learn they teach their parents. Providing the youth of New Hampshire with an agricultural awareness could pay off in large dividends in the future.

Isn't one of the goals of this association the promotion of your profession? What better way than becoming an active participant of the N.H. Agriculture in the Classroom Council? A representative from your association is welcome to attend meetings and bring your program suggestions. Providing some plant expertise to the Council just may result in an increased emphasis in the area of plant science. Offering touring opportunities to schools by your members surely will enhance the AITC program and help your industry through the exposure you will receive.

Yes, opportunity is knocking for you and your association. Hopefully, the sound will be heard and the door will be opened. Take a chance, walk through the opening and share your profession with the future.

Cal Schroeder is the Strafford County Extension Educator. For further information you can write Cal at this address: County Administration & Justice Building, Dover, NH 03820. Or call him at (603) 749-4445.

Marlborough Greenhouses: a Su

Your take a right after the post office, just past the Texaco station, and the third house on the right is a yellow clapboard Victorian with white trim set among mature plantings of shrubs and trees.

Behind it are the greenhouses—two plastic, three glass— tightly arranged on property of little over an acre.

It was called the Felsboro Gardens five-and-a-half years ago when Diane and Dale Lacasse bought it. It was a local landmark— a retail greenhouse and nursery operation that had been in business for fifty years. Dale and Diane planned to continue the business in the form in which it had always been— and they did so for three years. "We had over five hundred varieties," Diane said. 'We were good," Dale agreed.

But even the first year had given indications of how slow any growth would be—there was the limited acreage, the cost of oil, taxes (100% assessment). They looked at alternatives and they made a big decision: they became a mail order business—exclusively bulbs—from October to March. It was a risky step, but they've tripled sales by doing so. "And we expect another big jump this year," Dale said.

The first year's number of pans was small—350 8" pans, each containing "The Dutch Garden"— nineteen bulbs of five varieties—tulips, hyacinth jonquil, crocus, scilla—that would bloom in succession. They were still running the retail business then, but the start seemed promising and the following year they decided to concentrate on mail order bulbs only. It was a difficult decision ("It was really going against a town tradition," Dale said, but today their own customer list numbers 7500 and this year they will pot up 10,000 pans.

The old greenhouse no longer contain plants, but under one 30 x 96 plastic house is a 20 x 90 custom-made cooler "from Bush Refrigeration, out of New Jersey." The two layers of poly keep the weather off and, in winter, keeps the cooler from freezing. Liquid shade is used,

sprayed on the inside to prevent it from being knocked off by the snow. "We felt we had to move away from the traditional greenhouse," Diane said. "We were spending nine thousand for oil, now we spend one for electricity. We go with the weather. In

---

---

winter, we need to keep the bulbs cool; in summer, the coolers are empty."

Most aspects of the business are very precisely defined. There are two crops. The Christmas crop is the main one. The second is sent until March 15. After that, the coolers are emptied and next year's season is planned.

The only pot used is a white Kord 8: bulb pan with a matching saucer. The customer can have the pan placed in a hand-woven ashwood basket and 15% of the customers want just that.

Now there are variations in the type of bulb garden you can order. The most popular is still 'The Dutch Garden," but there are pans of tulips, and mixes of hyacinths and crocus as well. The hyacinth gardens can be blue, pink, or white, or mixed; the tulips come in red and apricot—clean, clear colors.

Choosing which tulips to use is not a simple task. Many factors are involved in the decision: the tulip has to pre-cool; it must have sturdy stems and the height should be no more than 18; the color must be attractive (strictly a subjective test); it should force within four weeks; the flower should last two. The LaCasses have checked out a couple dozen ("In winter, our house is full of tulips," Diane says), but they admit to being very fussy and have found only three that they've liked. They're trying to find a

ssful Transition Takes Place

really good white—and a yellow, but up to now, none of the bulbs have met their standards. So, again this winter, their home will be full of flowers.

The process begins around the first week in August, when seven yards of loam arrives and Dale mixes it with pro-mix (two parts pro-mix, one part loam), then steams the complete mix. He has an old Dillon steamer ("it never breaks down") and does two loads a day every day for the next couple months.

Four part-time workers are hired in October when the potting begins. (They work through March.) Everyone pots, but it's not assembly-line style—one person does a whole unit. There is an initial watering and spot watering after that.

But along with the potting, another aspect begins—the marketing side of things. "Advertising is key," Dale says. "You've got to have proper advertising."

This year, 7500 brochures will be mailed in October. The brochures are simple—"country"—with pen-and-ink drawings of the various pans of bulbs. They conform to outsiders' ideas of how quaint things are up here in New Hampshire and the response to them is very favorable.

But their major advertising is done in magazines. And it is crucial to choose the right ones—"With ads in the wrong places, you could lose your shirt." It's difficult to define the type of magazine in which their ads draw a sufficiently favorable response, but through trial and error, they've found a few which seem to work well. Each year they try ads in new publications and slowly, they are expanding the framework for their advertising.

Diane is in charge of the office; Dale is in charge of the packing. In the packing process, the pan is put into a box, florist grass is tucked around the tender shoots, and styrofoam peanuts are put around the entire unit.

The address labels have already been printed out by the office computer; in the packing room, as another computer weighs the

unit, Dale punches in the zip code, and a label with the correct postage on it is spit out. The packages are shipped through UPS and on a busy day, two hundred units go out.

Diane and Dale see the growth of the business tied to increased use of technology—the next step is

---

'Sitting with them on their porch in perfect August weather... I felt these people had already reached an early plateau of success'

---

to upgrade the computer systems in general.

Winters were their busy time; on summer days, they could linger and talk, their business was portable; technology would allow it to grow. Sitting with them on their porch in perfect August weather, with story-book clouds billowing above the green hills, I felt these people had already reached an early plateau of success.

Dale sensed what I was thinking. 'It's not as easy as it looks on a day like this," he said." It's a tricky business. In the greenhouse, things were more stable. If you worked hard, you'd have some success. But this is different—if you're not on top of things 100%, you could go belly-up. There are so many factors—gauging the mood of the public, getting the right ads in the right places...there could be a UPS strike... there are so many factors..."

I understood what he was saying, but as I thought about what I'd seen, Dale and Diane's choices seemed wise ones and worries aobut the future prosperity of Marlborough Greenhouses didn't enter my mind at all. (B.P.)

For further information: Dale and Diane La-Casse, Marlborough Greenhouses, Inc., P.O. Box 32, Marlborough, NH 03455; telephone: (603) 876-4397.

15

The Mitsubishi Fuso 4WD FG. Built to work where others can't.

There's always been a need for a four-wheel drive, cab-over light-duty truck that can conquer sand, snow, steep hills, and off-road conditions. A **real** truck.

The 127 HP, 11,600 lb./GVW, intercooled, turbocharged diesel, MITSUBISHI FUSO 4WD FG, is exactly that truck.

A cab-forward design with exceptional front and side visibility lets drivers see over, and around, snowplows. Up, and down, hilly terrain. And threatening conditions that conventional designs hide.

Wheelbase options help maintain the original design integrity that's often sacrificed by unnecessary adaptions.

A durable, reliable chassis, frame, and suspension system not only makes the ride smooth. But also protects the truck, the load, and your investment. And, accepts a variety of body and box options.

It is a truck that has survived over 5,000 miles of threatening conditions in the Australian outback to finish the 1988 Wynn's Safari Rally Race when 50% of the entrants didn't.

MITSUBISHI FUSO 4WD FG will work on those jobs that destroy ordinary, conventional trucks.

LIBERTY INTERNATIONAL
1400 South Willow Street
Manchester, NH 03103
Parts: 669-8524 623-8873
NH WATS: 1-800-562-3814

MITSUBISHI
FUSO

16

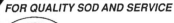

18

Pesticide License Renewal

As sure as the birds go south and we decorate for the holiday season at the end of the year another tradition is observed–renewing our Applicator's License.

Whether you consider this necessary function to be a breeze or not, the fact remains that without a current license in hand you will not be able to purchase restricted products–from a reputable and licensed dealer, that is.

To allow your State agency time to process your paperwork and issue your new license we suggest that you purchase your restricted chemicals prior to the expiration of your old license.

After years of dealing with this annual problem we just don't think we can look to our State agencies for a faster turnaround, especially when we hear that some are understaffed and short of funds.

The biggest tip we can give is–get your paperwork in on time. No license, no goods!

The 1991 All-America Selections Winners

All America Selections is a non-profit organization founded in 1932. Its mission is to test new, unsold cultivars grown from seed and to introduce those found to have significant horticultural value as AAS Winners.

All-America Selections is pleased to announce that ten new cultivars–an unusually bountiful crop–have been selected to receive the AAS Award for 1991. These are:

Gaillardia Pulchella 'Red Plume'
(AAS Flower Award Winner). 'Red Plume' has a dingle, uniform color, whereas other gaillardia flowers come in several colors and are available only in a color mixture. The plant is compact and branching, not needing the support other gaillardia types require.

Geranium F1 'Freckles'
(AAS Flower Award Winner). 'Freckles' flower umbels are large, containing a high-quality full flower head. A close look at each pink floret will reveal five petals, each with a rose freckle. Plants are compact and with a mounded habit.

Pansy 'Padparadja'
(AAS Flower Award Winner). The two-inch blooms of 'Padparadja' are a bright orance pumpkin color. The plant itself is only six inches high and will continue to bloom in full sun or semi-shade, in heat and humidity.

Vinca 'Pretty in Rose'
(AAS Flower Award Winner). 'Pretty in Rose' is a new color for vinca–it's a deep rose, almost purple. Blossoms of 1-2" in diameter are produced on 16"-high heat-and-drought tolerant plants.

Vinca 'Parasol'
(AAS Flower Award Winner). Twelve-inch high heat-and-drought tolerant plants produce large (1 1/2-2") white blossoms with red centers.

Vinca 'Pretty in Pink'
(AAS Flower and Bedding Plant Award Winner). 'Pretty in Pink' is the first pastel pink vinca. This is a color-breeding breakthrough. It was bred with germplasm of native species from Madagascar. Dr. Ronald Parker of the University of Connecticut bred this unique variety. The 12" plants are both heat and drought tolerant.

Pansy F1 'Maxim Marina'
(AAS Bedding Plant Award Winner). The flower is an unusual combination of light blue petals, shading to a velvety-blue face outlined in white.

The blooms are described as "enduring"–enduring heat and drought remarkably well.

Squash F1 'Tivoli'
(AAS Vegetable Award Winner). 'Tivoli' is an improved vegetable spaghetti squash. The plant has a compact bush habit; the squash matures in about 100 days and weighs 3-5 pounds.

Watermelon F1 'Golden Crown'
(AAS Vegetable Award Winner). 'Golden Crown' ripens to a rich golden yellow rind color when mature, making the fruit easy to locate among the vines. The melons (6-8 pounds, icebox size) mature early (eighty days from sowing seed) and the plants are tolerant to powdery mildew and anthracnose.

Bean 'Kentucky Blue'
(AAS Vegetable Award Winner). This new pole bean combines qualities from two of the most popular pole beans, 'Kentucky Wonder' and 'Blue Lake'. These vigorous vines produce round, straight pods of improved quality.

For further information, contact All-America Selections, 1311 Butterfield Road, Suite 310, Downers Grove, Illinois 60515. Telephone: (708) 963-0770.

21

22

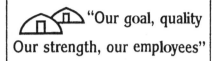

23

'A WESTON NURSERIES INTRODUCTION'

*Rhododendron PJM
(Hybridized in 1940)*

A phrase which stands for the very best that fifty years of horticultural innovation and testing can produce. Weston Nurseries is proud to have developed and introduced these outstanding plants for the benefit of the American Nursery Industry.

- Rhododendron PJM *(1940)**
- Rhododendron Henry's Red *(1958)**
- Rhododendron Shrimp Pink Hybrids *(1958)**
- Rhododendron Aglo *(1964)**
- Rhododendron Olga Mezitt *(1964)**
- Rhododendron Weston's Pink Diamond *(1964)**
- Rhododendron Molly Fordham *(1966)**
- Rhododendron Milestone *(1972)**
- Rhododendron April Snow *(1978)**

- Azalea Jane Abbott *(1942)**
- Azalea Vyking *(1958)**
- Azalea Pink and Sweet *(1963)**
- Azalea Parade *(1963)**
- Azalea Golden Showers *(1963)**
- Azalea Pink Clusters *(1972)**

*YEAR HYBRIDIZED

27

Special Requests

Lonnie Livingston of Portland, Oregon, has written, asking if we "have a staff horticulturist or anyone who could locate a Tree Peony." This is the small, hardy, deciduous Paeonia suffruiticosa tree of China and Japan.

Anyone who has information should send it to: Rare Plants, Lonnie Livingston, 8016 North Ida, #10, Portland, Oregon, 97203; telephone: (503)289-0069.

Also, the Plantgrowers' Association is looking for a member who is willing to serve on the Board of Directors of the Granite State Garden and Flower Show. Duties would involve planning and organizing the show held at the Man-chester Armory in early March.

Anyone interested should contact Chris Robarge, 56 Leavitt Road, Hampton, NH 03842. His work phone is (603)862-1074.

Special Thanks

The NH Plantgrowers' Association would like to give special thanks to Bob Butler of Butler-Florists & Growers Insurance Agency of New England, Inc., of Westborough, Massachusetts. He was unable to attend the summer meeting, but sent his regrets and included a contribution to the scholarship fund. Many thanks, Bob; hope you can make it next year.

The Association would also like to thank the members who contributed plant material to the New Hampshire Department of Agriculture's exhibition at the Eastern States Exposition in West Springfield, Massachusetts. The contributors include L.A. Brochu & Sons, Concord; Garden of Eves, Greenland; Gem Evergreen Company, Hooksett; Gold Star Wholesale Nursery, Canterbury; and Millican Nurseries, Chichester. Thanks to all of you.

The display, which is inside the building, is centered around a reproduction of the Cornish/Windsor covered bridge. There are two ponds and a natural planting. Over a million people visit the Eastern States Exposition each year.

1990 New Hampshire Plant Growers' Association Officers

President
Kirk Weyant
Gold Star Sod Farm
& Wholesale Nursery
Canterbury, NH 03224
783-4716

Secretary/Treasurer
Christopher Robarge
UNH/TSAS
Horticultural Facilities Manager
Durham, NH 03824
862-1074

Directors
Jennifer Gould
Phillips Exeter Academy
Exeter, NH 03833
778-0224

Tom Price
Meredith Gardens
RFD 1 Box 233
Center Harbor, NH 03226
284-7709

Alan Eves
Garden of Eves Greenhouse
192 Breakfast Hill Road

Greenland, NH 03840
436-3581

Richard Emerson
Emerson Avenue Greenhouses
181 Emerson Ave.
Hampstead, NH 03841
329-5525

Bruce Holmes
The Greenery of Ossippee
PO Box 1449
Wolfeboro, NH 03894
539-5995

NEW HAMPSHIRE PLANT GROWERS ASSOCIATION
THE PLANTSMAN EDITOR
UNH RESEARCH GREENHOUSES
DURHAM, NH 03824